Powerful Project Proposals:

Presenting to Big Shots!

By

Kathy O'Neal

Orlando, Florida

ISBN: 1-4033-4556-2 (Electronic)
ISBN: 1-4033-4557-0 (Softcover)

This book is printed on acid free paper.

1stBooks – rev. 07/05/02

This booklet is available at quantity discounts for bulk purchases of 500 or more.
For information, please call 321-939-0982, Monday – Friday,
10 am – 5:30 pm EST.
International calls: 011-01-321-939-0982.

Please visit our website at

www.accelerated-manager.com

Contents

Setting the Stage

McCreight, Thacker, Lampson, Sproull and Boggs—are these names familiar to you? Likely not. And yet, these five computer geniuses masterminded the single-most revolutionary technology that humankind has ever known.

What about names like Bill Gates and Steve Jobs? Oh yes, you likely recognize those famous "technology" names.

Well, let me tell you a story…a true story…about five people who, geniuses though they were, were unable to successfully "pitch" a most powerful project proposal to their company's top decision makers. Their lack of success forever changed our view of their company, and pushed their individual names into the dusty corners of "what could have been."

Where Were You in '72?

The year was 1972. Nixon gave a resounding thump to McGovern in the race for the White House. I was a college freshman, and got my first glimpse of a real computer.

Oh, I had seen a Wang desk-top calculator two years earlier. It was pretty snazzy! It took up "only" one full desktop, corner to corner, and it could add, subtract, multiply and divide with lightening speed! I was mesmerized.

But this current glimpse of advanced electronic machinery was even better! This was a **real** computer—the kind that had been used to send men to the moon just three years earlier. I was studying computer programming, and by accident got just a peek of the gargantuan electronic brain that lived in a large, private, climate-controlled room on the university campus in Columbia, Missouri.

"The Computer" was in a hush-hush, awe-inspiring environment. The Computer Room was tightly guarded by specially selected grad students and their computer science professors. On the hot summer Missouri days when The Computer would start to overheat, the grad students would rush into town to buy dry ice to pack around The Computer's hardware which was jam packed into that window-less room.

During this same time, there were five guys in a Palo Alto, California research center. They were scientists and engineers, kicking around ideas and experimenting with this concept: How can research be made more accessible to the common person?

Harnessing the Power

These five men—McCreight, Thacker, Lampson, Sproull and Boggs—had an idea: What if you could harness the power of those giant Computers and scale everything down to a device that was small enough to fit in an office comfortably…or maybe even on the top of a desk, such as Wang had done with his basic calculator?

Over the course of the early to mid-1970's, these five computer processing geniuses strategized just such a compact computer—a "personal" computer. They called their machine the "Alto" after the town where they worked. It consisted of four major parts: A keyboard similar to the set-up of typewriter keys, a disk storage/processor box, a graphics display screen, and a funny little device they called the "graphics mouse".

They had two main goals in making research more accessible to the common person: (1) To provide each user with a personal **computing** facility that could meet all of their individual needs, and (2) To provide a **communications** facility that would allow users to share information easily—to "network".

These five visionaries refined their amazing concepts, and in 1978 their organization donated 50 Altos to MIT, Carnegie Mellon, and Stanford University. These Alto machines became the standard against which other research technologies were judged.

Just One Problem

There was only one problem. These five brilliant men could not convince their employer of their creation's usefulness. They had the right idea, they had the passion, they had the dedication...but they just didn't know how to successfully present this very powerful project proposal to their company's Big Shots.

As smart as these five men were, they were unable to help their company's Big Shots complete the puzzle. As a result, the Big Shots concluded that the proposed project wasn't terribly practical—after all, they reasoned, there would <u>never</u> be a large-scale need for personal computers!

If the five geniuses had been better able to present their proposal, then the names of these five men might be logged into your memory banks instead of names like Bill Gates or Steve Jobs. And instead of Apple, Microsoft, or IBM, you would rightly and forever associate the technology that changed the world with Xerox Corporation. (Yep, Xerox!)

It may seem unfathomable that a company could have so much in its grasp: All the right ideas, the passion, the vision, the unparalleled opportunity…and still not attain the right conclusion.

Additional Skill Sets Required

And yet, I've personally seen other great ideas— ideas that could literally make companies (and their shareholders) millions and millions of dollars— languish in those same dusty corners of "what could have been" (and what <u>should</u> have been). These ideas languished because the gifted individuals who proposed them lacked the additional skill sets necessary to successfully present their powerful project proposals.

Don't fumble <u>your</u> future! In this guide, I'll reveal to you the profile of most Big Shots, and show how you can tap into this knowledge to make presentations that are impressive and effective. We'll also chat about additional tools, techniques, and tips on image enhancement to ensure your proposals reflect your thorough professionalism.

Picking up the additional skill sets necessary to present to Big Shots isn't all that hard. You just need a little inside information to get you started on the right foot.

So let's first get into the mind-sets of those Big Shots and see what makes them tick. Then we'll strategize how you can also use the other information in this guide to make powerful project proposals that Big Shots will be delighted to hear about, will quickly accept, and (most importantly) will eagerly fund!

Chapter 2

Profile of Mr./Ms. BigShot

Successfully presenting to Mr./Ms. BigShot takes three areas of concentration: Preparing yourself, preparing your delivery techniques, and leveraging the psychological angles that work well with Big Shots.

In this chapter, we'll focus on the psychological angles. Knowledge is power, so the more knowledgeable you are about how Big Shots think, the more easily you can get in-tune with them for your proposal presentation.

Mr./Ms. BigShot pays attention only to things that add value to BigShot's work day. Here's what most Big Shots consider to be of value:

- Big Shot wants to improve the company's bottom line (profitability).

- Big Shot wants to find, and be recognized for finding, solutions to problems.

That's pretty much it. Big Shots consider anything else to be a distraction at best, and an out-and-out waste of their time at worst.

Responsibility to Shareholders

In pursuit of these two ideas of value, Big Shots believe they have a responsibility to the company's shareholders to personally investigate new ideas and suggestions. This is good news! Big Shots actually want to hear new ideas and suggestions—IF presented appropriately.

Here's what you need to know first. Big Shots respond to ideas/suggestions that may lead to Shareholder Value. Now don't roll your eyes over the term Shareholder Value! The concept is really quite simple, and absolutely key to understanding what makes Big Shots tick. If it makes you feel better, substitute the term Company Value for Shareholder Value.

True Shareholder Value comes from one of the following:

- A sustained, controllable increase in Revenue.

- An appropriate lowering of Expenses—most often gained by improvements in the effectiveness/efficiency of workers or machinery.

- A combination of the above.

Hey, that's not difficult to grasp, is it? We want to either sell more, or produce our goods/services for less, or both. Piece of cake!

The funny thing is that these simple but important concepts are often overlooked by those who pitch proposals to Big Shots. The presenters get so wound up in the bells and whistles (features) of the proposed product/service, they often overlook what Big Shots value most: Impact on Revenue, impact on Expenses, or impact on both.

Don't Overlook Shareholder Value

You're not going to make the same mistake! I'm going to teach you to present your proposal in such a way that Mr./Ms. BigShot can easily connect its impact to Shareholder Value. Once you learn how to do this, you will see immediate positive results. You will focus on becoming a problem solver by clearly and confidently showing BigShot how to complete the puzzle.

Increase your confidence by remembering that Big Shots are always on the lookout for measurable improved results. Great ideas presented well are always of interest. You can confidently present powerful project proposals as Big Shot's business partner. No need to allow any difference in management levels to be a distraction.

Though many Big Shots appear to be intimidating and demanding, it helps to remember that they are people, too. They want to do their best for the company, the shareholders, the customers, and the employees. They also want to maximize pleasures and rewards for themselves and their families.

Gee, that sounds a lot like what I want to do, too. How about you?

Desired Opportunities

Let's remember that Big Shots are therefore interested most in project proposals that show opportunities like these:

- Increase Revenue, market share (especially new customers), and ultimately Shareholder Value via increased stock prices and/or dividends if issued.

- Increased efficiencies and effectiveness, especially for "front line" employees directly involved in Revenue generation and/or mission-critical processes.

- Protection of existing market share

- Expansion of add-on business from existing customers

- Getting products/services to market more quickly than the competition

- Reduction of fixed and variable Expense. If you're not familiar with fixed and variable expenses, just remember that Big Shot wants to appropriately reduce any type of Expense in a big way.

Now that we have a better understanding of what Big Shots are looking for, let's take a closer look at exactly who the Big Shots are in a company. Do you know who your BigShot truly is?

Will the Real BigShot Please Stand Up!

Usually Mr./Ms. BigShot is a CEO (Chief Executive Officer), President, or Chairman of the Board. But not always. Sometimes others, such as a key Vice President, may have the ultimate power in saying Yes or No to proposed projects. Why? Because BigShot VP is so well respected by those above him/her that the organization's leaders will not proceed with a new course of action if they perceive that BigShot VP objects to it.

Who is your true Big Shot? There is usually just one per organization or division. If you are still confused as to who your Big Shot is likely to be, ask this question: Who holds the checkbook? By that I mean: Who can approve the funding of this proposal? It's likely not the CFO (Chief Financial Officer). Someone else usually approves the project, perhaps with the advice of the CFO, but not at the direction of the CFO. When you figure out Who Holds The Checkbook, then you've got your Big Shot.

Depending upon the complexity and/or dollar-size of your project proposal (and your company), however, you may need to make your pitch to multiple Big Shots across various organizations. I once had to make 11 separate pitches of the same project proposal across multiple organizations in our global Fortune 100 company. Each of the 11 Big Shots held a piece of the Checkbook, and therefore any one of them could have squashed the project proposal. Fortunately, as the project's financial analyst & presenter, I was able to help all 11 Big Shots complete the puzzle. The project proposal was agreed to and funded by well over $100 Million. That's some bucks!

More Big Shot Psyche

How do I consistently get various project proposals funded? Well, here are a few more secrets. To fully understand these secrets, we're going to delve even deeper into the Big Shot psyche.

There are two additional key elements here. The first element is that BigShot must sense that you, the proposer, have the ability, responsibility and follow-through to make the proposal "happen." (I'll give you some tips on this later.) The second element is that BigShot is recognized as making the final decision—not you. (Yes, I know it's "your" proposal, but you're not going to get anywhere if you tightly hold on to that attitude.)

Your job is to show Mr./Ms. BigShot solutions in a way that s/he can easily understand, and then set-up the opportunity for Mr./Ms. BigShot to <u>select</u> a course of action. This selection will hopefully be along your lines of reasoning, but don't simply focus on your own personal view. It's overkill, and it's not your decision to make—it's BigShot's.

Intangible Victories

You see, in addition to the tangible Shareholder Values we already listed on page 8, there are also intangible "victories" for all Mr./Ms. BigShots. These intangible victories are secondary to the tangible Shareholder Values. They should never be used as substitutes for the tangible values, but can be quite effective when paired with them:

- Mr./Ms. BigShot wants to be recognized as a leader in the industry and in the community.

- Mr./Ms. BigShot wants a winning organization admired by all.

- Mr./Ms. BigShot often wants to gain greater power and control.

- Mr./Ms. BigShot wants to retain happy employees who are hard workers.

- Mr./Ms. BigShot wants greater peace of mind—less risk, less worry.

Mr./Ms. BigShot wants to talk to business people such as yourself who fully understand a business problem AND have realistic, well-thought out ideas for solving the problem. Then, Mr./Ms. BigShot wants to be appropriately recognized as being the one in charge to select the best solution by getting the chance to do just a little "hands-on" work with the proposal.   More on how you can create this opportunity later!

Characteristics of Big Shots

For now, let's continue by looking at some of Mr./Ms. BigShot's typical characteristics.   Do you recognize any of these in *your* BigShot(s)?

- Focused on the "big picture" and high-level company vision

- Passionate leadership and credibility

- Big ego, with many Big Shots still placing emphasis on power, authority, and control

- Willing to take calculated risks for a new idea with high upside potential

- Creative or able to recognize and appreciate the creativeness of others

- Decisive

Now here is a secret that many Big Shots don't want you to know about: Many Big Shots are not that good with detailed financials.

If you start presenting a lot of financial ratios and complex measurements, their eyes are gonna glaze over. They will be too embarrassed to admit that they don't "get it", and will be too scared to commit financial resources to your project because they don't see the direct, tangible connection to Shareholder Value.

You will have to help them complete the financial puzzle. Fear not: Accelerated help is here! Let's now turn to a Financial Primer re Big Shots so you'll know what to watch out for and how to work around it.

Financial Primer re Big Shots

In the last chapter, I shared that you may have to help your Big Shot complete the financial puzzle because many Big Shots are not really good with financials. If you, too, aren't good with financials, then quickly do yourself and your proposal a favor by linking up with a partner who is good at presenting financials in a simple manner. Financial analysts who can speak in layman's terms are around—they just likely aren't your company's CFO (Chief Financial Officer).

Hunt instead in the lower-to-middle management ranks in the financial organization, and perhaps start with someone who has a teaching background. Then, show them the section of Chapter 2 regarding examples of Shareholder Value, and this Chapter 3 as well.

Background of *Your* Big Shot

Hmmm? I sense that a few of my readers don't believe that many Big Shots are weak in financials. Well, then...I suggest you take a close look at the background of your Big Shot. If s/he came from a sales or marketing background, as Big Shots most often do, then you are in for a challenge with the very important financial piece of your proposal.

Why? It isn't that these folks aren't smart—they are very smart, and they are often charismatic leaders to boot! However, Big Shots with a strong sales/marketing background have seldom been forced to calculate profitability from end-to-end. You see, the focus in their Sales/Marketing organizations was upon strictly Revenue, and what Revenue stimulations alone cost. The rest of the profitability equation—such as expense in the Operations organization—is therefore a bit fuzzy in the minds of many.

Now those few Big Shots with either a financial or operations background already know that Profitability is the true name of the game. A pitch on, for example, an Expense reduction proposal will be a lot easier to them. However, since such a proposal doesn't increase Revenue, you're going to have to gently lead the BigShot with a sales/marketing background regarding profitability in order to gain his/her attention.

Just in case your financial background could use a brush-up, let's start with a simple profitability formula:

Profit = Revenue – Expenses

If you remember those three Shareholder Value ideas identified on page 7 (it's okay to look back), you can dovetail those ideas with Profit. If your proposal increases Revenue a lot without increasing Expenses by very much, then you've got a winning idea. If the Revenue stays the same, and the Expenses go down significantly for a good reason, then you've also got a winning idea. Or, you've got a really fabulous idea if a combination of both of those can occur without significant risk.

Financial Fallacies

But here's the rub: Some Big Shots, especially those with sales/marketing backgrounds, assume that anytime the Revenue goes up, so does profitability. It doesn't.   Profitability is also dependent upon Expenses.   If the way in which Revenue goes up triggers a high rise in Expenses, Profits could go down, even to the point of losing money with each additional sale.

Some Big Shots even assume that if Revenue isn't going up, then a proposed Expense reduction investment for that area isn't worth listening to. That assumption is wrong as well.   A change which significantly drops Expense in an area with flat Revenue often boosts Profit far better than any Revenue stimulation.

Both the Revenue and the Expense pieces must be looked at to properly gauge the impact on Profit. Here is a simple example, and for this purpose, the terms "cost" and "expense" are synonymous.

PizzaBoy Ownership

Let's say you are the new owner of PizzaBoy, an existing pizzeria in your town. You are wondering if profit could be improved if you stayed open one hour later on Thursday nights, like many of the retail stores in the area. You decide to try it, and instruct your pizza maker (who also acts as cashier and closing manager in the final hours) to stay open an extra hour this Thursday, from 9 pm to 10 pm.

The next day, the pizza maker tells you that he sold two pizzas between 9 pm and 10 pm. One sold for $8.50 and the other sold for $9.50. What was your profit from staying open that one hour later?

Now, most Big Shots with a sales/marketing background will tell me that Profit was increased by $18.00 (from $8.50 + $9.50) that hour.

A financial/operations Big Shot will more likely give me the correct answer, which is this: Kathy, I don't know what Profit was made because you haven't given me any Expense information.

Did you fall for the $18.00 fallacy? If so, don't worry about it—you can still become a BigShot, because most of them would have missed this, too. They mistakenly call this $18 the Profit—but it isn't Profit, it is just the Revenue. Revenue alone does not equal Profit!

Okay, now let's continue on, because you really need to understand additional financial fallacies that many Big Shots have. That way, you can gently lead them around their mistaken assumptions.

Let's go back to our PizzaBoy example. Now I'll give you the Expense information—we'll keep it simple. You'll have to do just a little addition and subtraction—nothing more. You'll need to think about Labor (the pizza maker's pay), Raw Materials (dough ingredients and sauce, cheese and other toppings), and Utilities (extra electricity for the pizza oven and lights being on for an additional hour).

Identifying Expense

Usually the pizza maker gets $8/hour, but since he's working overtime for that additional hour, he gets paid time-an-a-half…that comes to $12 for the extra hour of Labor. The Raw Materials for the $8.50 pizza costs $3.50, and the Raw Materials for the $9.50 pizza costs $4.50. The extra Utilities for the additional pizza oven time and lights comes to $5.00.

Now let's see what happens. I like to add up all the Expenses first. That means: $12 + $3.50 + $4.50 + $5. That totals $25 of Expense for the additional hour. Now let's plug and chug into our Profit formula.

$$Profit = Revenue - Expense$$

Profit = $18 - $25   Hmmm…that equals a loss of $7!

Hey, maybe staying open an extra hour on Thursday night isn't such a good idea. Or is it? Now see, at this point, the people with sales/marketing background are screaming at me, "Kathy, I just need to advertise! I'll stimulate my sales that hour on Thursday night by letting my customers know that I'm staying open later."

How About an Ad?

OK, we'll check that idea out. You place an ad in your local paper on Sunday specifically pointing out that you are now open one additional hour on Thursday nights. The next Thursday night rolls around, and the pizzeria again stays open until 10 pm. The pizza maker reports to you on Friday morning that sales did indeed increase between 9 pm and 10 pm Thursday night. A total of four pizzas were sold then: Two for $8.50 each and two for $9.50 each.

Now by this time both you and the sales/marketing BigShots know that the amount of Profit made that hour was NOT $36. That's because you know that $8.50 + $8.50 +$9.50+ $9.50 is merely the Revenue, not the Profit. What was the profit?

Oh, so maybe you never liked this kind of word problem in school? Okay, I'll help you out a little bit. How much was the Labor for that extra hour? Still $12 for that one hour, even though the pizza maker made and sold four pizzas. How much were the Utilities? Still $5 for that hour, even though a total of four pizzas were baked in the oven.

Now how about the expense of the Raw Materials? That's just a bit of calculation, because you had expenses of $3.50 + $3.50 + $4.50 + $4.50. So, the total Raw Material Expense was $16.

How much profit was made? If you tell me $3, don't worry, you can still be a BigShot because many of them would have come up with that wrong answer as well. The correct answer is: Kathy, I don't know what Profit was made because you haven't given me <u>all</u> of the Expense information.

The Missing Expense Item

What's missing? Yes, the sales/marketing folks do have an advantage here: They very likely realize that the cost of the advertisement used to stimulate Thursday's late night sales is missing. OK, I'll tell you that the cost of that advertisement was $15.

Hmmm, pizza sales doubled to four, and Revenue doubled to $36 with a $15 advertisement. Some Big Shots will tell me that's an additional $18 for a $15 ad—that's not bad, is it, Kathy?

Let's go back and look at the ENTIRE equation again—you must gently get the Big Shots to think end-to-end.

Profit = Revenue − Expense (all the Expense!)

Expense = $12 Labor + $16 Raw Material +
$5 Utilities + $15 Ad

Expense = $48

Profit = $36 - $48   (ooops…lost $12)

Hmmm…instead of losing just $7 as on the first Thursday night, the second Thursday night lost $12. Looks like a doubling of Revenue doesn't automatically guarantee any Profit at all!

Now you and I know that advertising takes a while to work, so it's possible that a well thought out ad campaign would eventually stimulate enough business from 9 pm – 10 pm on Thursday nights to turn a profit for that hour. Maybe Yes and maybe No.

The point of the exercise is this. Many Big Shots are weak when it comes to financials. They assume incorrectly that a doubling in Revenue will always lead to favorable Profit. They also incorrectly assume that a process with flat Revenue is never worth additional investment. If these assumptions are not correct for your proposal, it's up to you to gently show Mr./Ms. BigShot that his/her assumption is…well, wrong.

A Little Secret

I'll tell you a true story, but don't let the BigShots at AT&T know that I told you this. It will just be our little secret.

At one of the successful AT&T business units where I used to work, our BigShot had a very strong sales & marketing background.   He was a truly charismatic, visionary leader who was very savvy about Revenue and the marketplace.   But he didn't have a clue about either Operations nor Finance, and as a result, he had a tough time grasping the monthly overall financials.

During the Controller's presentation, he would often ask, "Should I be happy or sad about that (financial measure)?" The Controller finally got to the point of including small up and down arrows at the end of each financial line to show BigShot which way each measure should be trending.

That little secret, however, is topped by a tale from two of my financial buddies at a division of Hewlett Packard. Facing a similar situation of non-financial BigShots, they insist they had to resort to "happy" and "frownie" faces throughout their monthly financial presentations. Otherwise, many of their BigShots were lost once the discussion got past the Revenue measures.

If you know of any similar "helps" in your company, would you please e-mail that info to me at kathy@accelerated-manager.com? I like to keep track of what works and what doesn't work in helping BigShots understand financial measures.

Anyhow, never assume that Mr./Ms. BigShot could correctly calculate the Profit made at PizzaBoy from 9 pm – 10 pm on Thursday nights…unless you know for sure that your BigShot has a strong financial background!

Chapter 4

Profile of Business People Successful at Presenting to Big Shots

In Chapter 2 we reviewed a profile of Mr./Ms. BigShot, and you may have seen some major commonalities to yourself. That's good—it's easier to present to people whom you view as similar to yourself.

People who are successful at presenting to Big Shots have a profile that is very likely similar to yours. Do you want to do your best for the company, the shareholders, the customers, and the employees?

How about maximizing pleasures for yourself and your family? Being recognized as a leader in a winning organization? Willing to take calculated risks? Dedicated and decisive?

Great! You've got the right stuff! Now all that's needed is to hone a few specifics in preparing yourself, and then later in preparing your delivery techniques.

Let's start with some easy specifics on proposal environment Dos and Don'ts. This may require you to do things just a little differently from what you're used to doing with your colleagues. We'll start with the Don'ts first.

Don't Do Small Talk. Big Shots have a timeframe that is shorter than yours and mine—every minute of their time is very valuable. Therefore, your proposal presentation will have to run according to a new and accelerated timeframe: Big Shot timeframe.

Don't try to "break the ice" with Mr./Ms. BigShot. Get right down to business and talk about your proposal and how it is the solution to a problem. When you're done talking business, if time allows, then you can do a small amount of chitchat to end on a positive note—just don't overdo it.

Don't Set False Expectations. Better to be shot down initially than to create false expectations that you (or your colleagues) can't live up to later. Don't make inflated nor exaggerated statements—you and your career are in this for the long haul!

Your business rapport and potential business partnership with BigShot will rely heavily on your projection of honesty and integrity. Remember that BigShot will be sizing you up as to whether you have the ability, responsibility, and follow-through necessary to make this proposal happen.

Don't Criticize Surroundings. Don't criticize anyone or anything related to BigShot's environment. That garish, ugly coffee mug may have been made by BigShot's son. The uncomfortable chair you're sitting in may have been chosen by BigShot's daughter. Just grin and bear it.

<u>Don't Share Inappropriate Confidential Information</u>. You already know you're not to tell trade secrets nor share "company private" information outside your company. In a similar manner, be very cautious about sharing company gossip with BigShot. Why? When asked what traits executives look for in their hiring process, the top two traits consistently sought are Honesty and Integrity.

If you spill negative secrets that you don't have the need or authority to share, you won't gain trust nor earn points with BigShot. For his/her question will always become: What's stopping you from betraying sensitive organizational information elsewhere in the company?

Here is a true story. We had a mid-level manager named Sally in our Public Relations organization. She was constantly slipping negative internal gossip to the company executives. If an employee criticized an executive's decision in a private e-mail (yikes!) and that e-mail came Sally's way, you can rest assured that Sally made a point to send it to the referenced executive.

My guess is that Sally thought she was gaining points in the eyes of the executives by negatively exposing some of her colleagues. But her scheme backfired.

When the layoff came, Sally was the first one shown the door. Seems the executives collectively perceived her as a troublemaker who purposely "stirred the pot". Since they could no longer trust her discretion with internal information, they also became concerned at having her in a Public Relations position.

You may or may not agree with their decision—but the fact remains that Sally found her point tally was negative with the execs.

<u>Don't Ask Who Else is Needed</u>. Don't ask Mr./Ms. Bigshot something like, "Who else do you need to get involved in making this decision?" That's like a slap in the face to Mr./Ms. BigShot. Remember that they like being recognized as the final decision maker, and will likely respond to such a question with, "No one! I alone decide!" Now you've got him/her riled up, and your business rapport just went down the drain...and likely with it, your proposal as well.

Instead, do you homework before you get to BigShot to find out if someone else's approval or advice will likely be sought. If you've overlooked someone, you won't need to ask. Mr./Ms. BigShot will eventually ask you, "Have you run this by BigShot VP? I'd like her/his consideration of this idea before I make my final decision." (Note that BigShot still declares authority for making the final decision.)

<u>Don't Assume Personal Rapport</u>. Don't ever assume that just because you've successfully established a business relationship with Mr./Ms. BigShot you are now entitled to personal rapport with him/her. Some Big Shots, especially female executives, lead very private lives outside the business world. They do not want their two worlds to intertwine.

<u>Don't Show Up Late</u>. Showing up late sends the message that you place little or no value on BigShot's precious time. This is the kiss of death to the business relationship. Do whatever you have to do to arrive on time <u>and</u> be ready to go. No excuses!

<u>Don't Ask for a Favor</u>. Hey, you're there to offer Mr./Ms. BigShot a solution to a problem—not to ask for a favor. This is not the time to be personally greedy nor cocky. When it comes to a business relationship, it's always best to have BigShot offer a favor rather than have you prematurely ask for one.

Now let's review our list of Don'ts:

- Don't do small talk
- Don't set false expectations
- Don't criticize surroundings
- Don't share inappropriate confidential information
- Don't ask who else is needed
- Don't assume personal rapport
- Don't show up late
- Don't ask for a favor

Got those under your belt? Okay! Then let's move on to the Dos.

<u>Do Make a Great First Impression</u>. This cannot be overemphasized! Remember the old saying, "You only get one chance to make a first impression." It's

true, and with BigShot's accelerated timeframe, it is more important than ever. It is so important that I've devoted an entire chapter later on how to present a truly polished, professional image—lots of little tricks to help you out.

You will need to use every tip, trick and tactic at your disposal. If each one helps by only 1 – 2 %, then stringing 5 or 6 of them together will boost your odds of success considerably. Don't overlook this later chapter.

For now, remember the one main key to success in this area: Avoid anything in dress or manner that will cause a distraction. Your proposal deserves BigShot's attention—not your jangling charm bracelet nor your garish plaid suit nor the fly you forgot to zip up (and yes, I have seen that happen).

As important as the first few seconds are, the last few seconds are important as well. Don't blow your entire proposal by doing something inappropriate afterwards. I once saw a presenter who ended an otherwise adequate talk by pulling out the lost, dirty underwear of a friend in the room. The presenter thought it was a clever joke. Bad move. Don't ever try to execute a "cute joke" with BigShot. Do remain a well-mannered professional throughout the entire proposal time.

Do Follow-Through. As to follow-through, do what you say you will do, and be willing to go above and beyond. If you've told Mr./Ms. BigShot that you'll send over additional info, then do so promptly and completely. Go the extra mile with perhaps a brief phone call to ensure that the info was received and understood. Be prepared to make sure you shine during this additional contact.

Do Make Noticeable Self Improvements. Here's another secret that many non-executives don't understand. Most Big Shots rise to top positions of importance and influence because they are on a constant self-improvement journey. This may be with traditional education, or via self-improvement programs, or a combination of both. Big Shots believe that constant progress and self-development are key characteristics to increasing a business person's value.

Therefore, never let yourself become intellectually, emotionally, nor physically stagnant. Need to lose weight? Do it. Need a higher formal education? Start on it—you'll likely get brownie points for being enrolled, even if your degree completion date is far down the road. Need additional industry/trade knowledge? Begin reading the industry/trade journals and periodicals that Big Shots read.

When you make your proposal, your self-improving background and resulting confidence will demonstrate that you, too, are upwardly mobile.

Do Choose an Upbeat Attitude. Everyone appreciates a winning attitude, especially Big Shots. Constant whiners and negative thinkers remain in the lower echelons of the corporate world, and Big Shots know it. Therefore, show Mr./Ms. BigShot that you know how to make the best of every situation.

Enthusiasm, a positive outlook, and graceful manners will take you a long, long way.

Most Big Shots know the importance of teamwork these days. Inclusive leadership skills are becoming more common, thank goodness. It is therefore important for you to show Mr./Ms. BigShot that you, too, appreciate the importance of the home team. Be sure to acknowledge the contributions of others in your project proposal to BigShot.

If you need buy-in from others in the organization, you'll help gain their approval by turning them/their department into heroes in BigShot's eyes. It doesn't have to be anything major, just something truthful. Swallow your pride, if need be, and compliment them briefly during your presentation. This works!

It also helps you display unshakable confidence in yourself and your solution when you are willing to share the credit. The more I gave credit away throughout my career, whether in proposals or general management situations, the more I seemed to gain in return.

Every Big Shot's team has room for another player IF that player is a "giver", not a "taker". Be looked upon as an asset, not a liability. "Liabilities" are quickly removed from the team, as in the plight of Sally, the office "tattler".

Speak and Write Well. The proper use of words, whether verbally or in charts or in a project document, provides us with key tools that we need to make a great and lasting impression.

Here is one of the best tricks you will ever learn for making superb presentations: Don't overwhelm Big Shots with fancy, technical jargon and a myriad of acronyms. (Engineers especially, please take note!)

Use plain and simple English. Make sure charts or hand-outs are letter perfect. (Proofread!) If you're not good at spelling, have someone else proofread your work before you present it to BigShot. Then, go back to school to brush up on your basic spelling skill sets. (Remember the "Do Make Noticeable Improvements" section.)

I have seen a lack of spelling/writing skills stall the careers of several lower level managers who otherwise would have been candidates for promotion.

The first time I encountered it, I was a fairly new supervisor assigned to my third work group. There was a very fine employee named Marge who had been stuck on the lower management rung for decades. Marge was about to retire.

I had been told verbally by Marge's prior supervisor that she would have been considered for a promotion long ago had she not been such a poor speller. This was back in the 1970's, and our company had no required career management documentation process at that time. I saw no notations in Marge's records that anyone had ever mentioned the need for better spelling to her.

So, I spoke to her privately and asked her straight out, "Marge, do you understand why you were never promoted further?" She told me, pleasantly, that no, she never understood why. But on the eve of her retirement departure, she would really like to know the reason.

When I told her it was because of her lack of spelling skill, she initially looked surprised, and then she grinned. Marge said that it had never occurred to her that it was something so simple. She knew she didn't spell well, but she didn't realize it was that important. (Big mistake on her part.)

She also reflected that she wished one of her prior supervisors had shared this information with her long ago. (Big mistake on their part that they didn't.) Marge said she would have been glad to go back to school for a course or two if she had realized it would directly help her chances of career success. I believe she would have, indeed.

Since then, I've counseled several other lower-rung managers about this same need. Unfortunately, none of them took my advice to improve their spelling skills, as they perceived there wasn't a need to do so in a financial organization. (Big mistake, unless you simply want to cling to the lower levels of accounting/finance forever and ever.)

Poor spellers: Please remember that your success depends on choice, not chance. Adjust your thinking accordingly before you wind-up like Marge…wondering why more promotions didn't happen.

Remember what we talked about in the "Do Make a Great First Impression" section? The one main theme regarding success in that area is to avoid anything that will cause a distraction from your proposal.

Well, then, don't allow your lack of spelling/writing skills to become a distraction to your project proposals. You want Mr./Ms. BigShot focused on your ideas, not distracted by your basic mistakes with the English language.

<u>Show That You Are Listening</u>. Few people *appear* to listen well. They may or may not listen well, but the point is that they are perceived by Big Shots to not listen with rapt attention to BigShot's words.

Listening with rapt attention in BigShot's world means that you are looking at BigShot when BigShot talks—not down at the table, not down at your feet, not fiddling with your papers, not looking at your watch, nor at the delivery man who just walked down the hallway.

When Mr./Ms. BigShot talks, you need to not only listen—you need to *appear* to listen as well. I learned this from being in a reverse position.

Once I had a boss who liked to listen with her eyes closed. I found this unnerving, though I was told by my peers that this was her modus operandi. As she was the boss, not I, I learned to put up with it. But, I never got comfortable with her doing this, and certainly wouldn't recommend you doing it with BigShot. Instead of him/her assuming you are in deep concentration, s/he may assume you are becoming bored and sleepy. Don't go there.

A little known secret about me is that I sometimes have trouble hearing out of my right ear. I have a suspected case of mild dyslexia, which seems to worsen with stress. As a result, over the years I've picked up some ability in reading lips in order to override the garbled words occasionally "heard" by my dyslexic right ear.

While some may classify my dyslexia as a slight disability (as I used to consider it myself in my teens), this slight abnormality has actually become a positive factor in presenting to Big Shots. It forces me to listen as closely as I can with my ears, <u>and</u> with my eyes. Big Shots feel special because I am *clearly* giving them my undivided attention.

Now let's review our list of Dos:

- Do make a great first impression
- Do follow-through
- Do make notable self improvements
- Do choose an upbeat attitude
- Do speak, write and spell well
- Do show that you are listening

Hey, those Dos and Don'ts aren't so hard, are they? Let me assure you—if you follow those Dos and Don'ts consistently, you'll be better than over half of those presenting project proposals today.

Next we'll turn to four advanced areas. Fear not, though! Knowledge is power, and you'll just need to put in a little time on these four, and perhaps a little money on one of them. (Fair warning!)

Chapter 5

The Big Shots' Secret Fears

Intimidating though your Big Shot may be, you'll be ahead of the game if you realize that all Big Shots have two common fears. These two fears were described by Anthony Parinello in his book Selling to VITO, and I totally agree with Anthony. Here are the biggest fears of a Big Shot:

Fear # 1: You are going to waste his/her precious time.

Fear # 2: Your conversation will include topics or phrases that are unfamiliar (techno-babble, uncommon acronyms, etc.)

These are very important fears to be aware of, because (to paraphrase Anthony) Mr./Ms.BigShot realizes that during a presentation, it's your job to talk, and his/her job to listen. As the presenter, you just have to make sure that BigShot doesn't finish his/her job before you do!

That's not easy, given that many Big Shots are poor listeners, especially if the presentation isn't structured exactly to his/her liking. Research has shown that you have literally less than 10 seconds to grab BigShot's attention. So don't dawdle—start right in.

Here's another little trick. Don't periodically ask, "Are there any questions?" Some Big Shots believe that answering this question with a "yes" makes them look stupid. (Hey, I don't agree with that, but that's not the point—the point is how *they* feel about it.)

So ask instead, "Have we covered this item to your satisfaction?" Or even saying, "What questions do you have?" is better than, "Are there any questions?" It throws the emphasis back on you as the presenter to make sure that the information is clearly understood.

Seek to Connect

You'll need to be sensitive to counteract the Big Shots common fears of wasted time and unfamiliar phrases. I learned this the hard way.

I had just been promoted to a financial analyst. I was to give a talk to several high rollers on the economic methods used in our group. I assumed the high rollers had economic backgrounds, and sought to dazzle them initially with my "economic brilliance".

I started my presentation with the comparison of two differing economic theories, and then went into some specific "bifurcated" data results. Imagine my surprise when one of the men gently said, "Do you realize that we haven't understood a word you've said for the past five minutes?"

Aaagghhh! What a silly, silly new analyst I was. I was trying to impress these two, rather than making an effort to connect with them in order to help them. I hadn't even asked what their specific economic needs were.

At that point, I had to stop my presentation, sit down with them and do what I should have done to begin with—assess their needs for the information, and present it in words that would be easy for them to understand.

As it turns out, neither of them had much economic background at all. Therefore, I had to toss out the rest of my presentation right then and there! What should I do now? This was my only chance, as they had traveled far to hear me, and would not be returning.

Falling back on what has since helped me over and over and over again in my career, I began to gently teach them. Not with fancy financial terms, but with the language I used in my prior career of teaching high school math.

Gentle Teaching, With Respect

If used with the proper respect for your audience's intellect (after all, these high rollers were very smart—they just hadn't been exposed to project economics), gentle teaching in layman's terms is one of the best, yet most seldom used powerful tactic in presenting project proposals.

A second tactic, just as important, is that the body of your presentation must start with what Big Shots see as benefits—the Shareholder Value focus—not the features that so many presenters focus on in error. Let's now look at this second tactic in more detail.

Chapter 6

Focus on Benefits vs. Features

Sharon was one of the smartest people I have ever met. She was a highly respected financial analyst in the communications network engineering organization of our Fortune 100 company. She had been involved in a very high dollar project proposal for three years. Though the project could save the company literally millions and millions of dollars per year in Labor expense, Sharon and the project's engineer just couldn't get the project approved.

After presenting the proposal repeatedly for the past two years, Sharon was ready to move on. I had just been promoted from another department to be her replacement. We had been given some time for cross-training.

Sharon walked me through the best designed and most intricate giant financial spreadsheet I had ever seen. It had been honed and refined over that three year period, and it was absolutely brilliant.

Everything was there in meticulous detail from a financial perspective. The project appeared to me to be a clear winner. The engineering organization felt so as well, and kept pushing the proposal over and over and over again to any relevant Big Shots who would listen. I couldn't understand why the project hadn't been approved in all this time. Over two dozen presentations had been made on this proposal over the past few years, but no approval had been given, and hence no funding.

Remember the Alto!

One such presentation was scheduled right before Sharon's departure. She knew her stuff cold, as she had been the financial analyst on the project proposal from the beginning. But as she got up to present, she leaned over to me and whispered, "Now you'll see my weakness—I just can't present."

She was right. Her presentation was awful. Even I, a strong supporter by now of both her and the project, was bored after about two minutes. By the five minute mark, she had totally confused and lost the entire audience—including the Big Shot.

She and her engineer partner had a great idea, and the passion, dedication, and vision to go with it. The engineer's presentation was fine, but without a strong financial presentation focusing on Shareholder Value, the Big Shot simply couldn't complete the puzzle. All that the Big Shot saw was a huge price tag and a very complex engineering concept.

What went wrong? A number of things. Let's focus on the toughest one first.

Wrong Focus

Sharon was focusing on the project's features, not its benefits. Now what do I mean by that? In this case, she was dovetailing with the engineer's project description—and focused on how much each major piece of hardware/software cost and why it cost so much. Lots of techno-babble and financial-babble in excruciating detail, as well as a bunch of engineering acronyms.

Guess what? None of that adds value to Mr./Ms. BigShot's day. It brings in Fear #2 (techno-babble, unfamiliar terms) which then leads to Fear #1 (this is a waste of my time). BigShot doesn't care that this is the best networking widget in the communications world and is therefore worth all this money to produce and install because it has all sorts of wonderful features.

What Mr./Ms. BigShot cares about is this: How and to what extent could this proposed project improve our current Shareholder Value? Increased revenue? Increased market share? New customers? Increased efficiency/effectiveness, and therefore a big reduction of expense? How would such a project increase the bottom-line of profitability?

Those are the benefits that Mr./Ms. BigShot wants to hear about. If there are enough clearly identified upside benefits to the project, without an undue amount of risk, then BigShot will likely say "yes". Trust me, s/he will.

Unfortunately, Sharon's presentation didn't focus on the very strong benefits of the project. She was down in the minutia of the features, as well as portraying just about every financial ratio and measurement known to economists—but not to most Big Shots.

Presentation Techniques

As you might suspect, Sharon's basic verbal presentation skills weren't good either. She spoke with a monotone, reading from her papers. And, possibly owing to the dozens of failed presentations, she certainly didn't display a positive, upbeat attitude.

Starting Over

Keeping the engineer's portion of the presentation, and utilizing the same financial information Sharon had, I created a whole new financial analysis presentation. This new presentation focused on the Shareholder Value benefits of increased efficiencies and effectiveness of front line employees, and the resulting reduction of a vast amount of labor expense accordingly. Bottom-line: Big opportunity for lots of additional Profit, with very little risk!

Never once did I mention why the new widgets (telecom switches) were so expensive at $5 million each. Nobody cares as long as the resulting implementation can truly save the company hundreds of millions of dollars per year, and take that savings (in this case, Labor) to the bottom line of profitability without a lot of risk.

Instead of seeing just a big project price tag and a complex engineering project, now the BigShots were able to complete this puzzle:

Puzzle: How can we save over a billion dollars in labor expense throughout the next ten years…thereby increasing our profitability by that same amount…without a lot of risk?

The BigShots' Conclusion: Why, we'll simply create and install these proposed new telecom switches. We've created and installed other new switches before, so there really is very little risk involved to a company with our telecom switch history.

Then, of course, a few of the more open BigShots admitted, "Hey, we should have approved this project two years ago. What are we waiting for?" Not only did the project get funding, it got funding at an accelerated pace.

Did the idea change? No. Were the financials any better? No. Was the new presenter's passion for the project any higher than her predecessor's? No.

The only thing that changed was the presentation itself…its focus, and also the delivery techniques. But the best delivery techniques in the world won't make up for a presentation that is severely lacking in Big Shot focus on benefits/Shareholder Value.

You've got the idea now, don't you? Good for you! Then, read on—more presentation tips, tricks, tactics and techniques are just around the corner.

Chapter 7

Encountering The Checker

It's unfortunate, but because all Mr./Ms. BigShots have previously had their valuable time wasted (Fear #1) by unfocused, unprepared, unprofessional project proposers, Big Shots often use a person I call The Checker.

I call him/her The Checker because the better ones have a checklist of what they believe should be in a suitable project proposal to BigShot. Therefore, think of The Checker's function as weeding out project proposals that are "not ready for prime time!"

If you are preparing a proposal for Mr./Ms. BigShot, you will likely encounter The Checker at some point— usually before you are "allowed" to present to BigShot.

Rule #1 in Encountering The Checker: Do not tick-off The Checker, especially in the initial encounter(s). The Checker can actually play an important role in the end-to-end decision making process, though they are <u>not</u> a true decision-maker. Repeat after me: Checkers are <u>not</u> true decision-makers, even though many of them will waste your valuable time in trying to prove to you they are in the decision-maker's seat.

They aren't—that's BigShot's job. Think of The Checker more as someone who can, especially if ticked-off, throw any number of obstacles and time delay tactics your way. That's not to say you can't eventually get around such stall tactics, but why go through all that additional negative time and energy if the bulk of it can be avoided?

Such hassles can be avoided (or at least reduced) once you understand what most Checkers perceive as his/her functions, and what the profile of most Checkers looks like.

Profile of The Checker

The Checker goes by different titles in different organizations. Most are in the lower to middle part of the management hierarchy. Checkers are usually highly educated, often with advanced and/or technical degrees and background (MBA's, engineers, computer science specialists).

Checkers are usually very analytical, and they just love to gather data, data, and more data. They crave knowledge for all sorts of facts, figures, functions and features of the widget (or service) included in your upcoming project proposal. They honestly believe they need all this data at their fingertips in order to properly inform Mr./Ms. BigShot how the project proposal is progressing.

However, The Checker doesn't want to be forced into making an overall final decision about any of this. Checkers are very risk-adverse, and are privately scared of actually recommending approval of *any* project proposal—for what if Mr./Ms. BigShot hears the proposal, then shoots it down for some reason that The Checker didn't see first? Then The Checker would feel (rightly or wrongly) as though s/he had failed in her/his gatekeeper responsibility.

The Checker doesn't want to feel like a failure. Who does?!! This is especially true for The Checker who is very loyal to Mr./Ms. BigShot, as many of them are. The Checker wants to be "A Hero" in Mr./Ms. BigShot's eyes, believing that s/he as The Checker is there to protect BigShot's valuable time.

The Checker's Focus

However, because most Checkers love gathering data much more so than making a recommendation about a project (which would require a decision, and hence risk, on their part), The Checker instead tries to tie up your precious time by focusing on two things:

1. The Checker will try to impress upon you how important The Checker is, and how s/he is intimately tied-in to the decision-making process. This is because s/he supposedly has BigShot's ear. Actually, I've found that Checkers are seldom tied to BigShot's final decision about a project, but many Checkers are indeed partial gatekeepers to their BigShot's schedule, so do remember Rule #1. (You do remember Rule #1 for Encountering The Checker, don't you? If not, go back and look at the first part of this chapter.)

2. The Checker will request lots of data from you…then more data…then more data…while insisting that s/he must understand every

46

working nuance of your proposed widget before your project proposal is ever "allowed" to reach BigShot.

What I find the most interesting part in Encountering The Checker is how long it takes him/her to get beyond his/her tunnel-vision of the **features** of a widget to the **benefits** of the project being proposed. I find this interesting because, as we discussed before, most BigShots don't care about the detailed features of the widget—they only care about the bottom-line (Shareholder Value) benefits of what the project has to offer. I guess that's why they are the BigShots and why The Checkers are…well, Checkers.

Your Choices

You have two choices when Encountering The Checker. Before you make your choice, remember that The Checker truly wants to be "A Hero" in BigShot's eyes. Unfortunately, most Checkers believe this means they need a detailed understanding of the widget's features rather than the project's benefits. Merely understanding features goes along with The Checker's love of data, data, and more data.

Many project proposers/presenters try as much as possible to avoid The Checker. While it's highly desirable for the proposer to subtly control the situation so that The Checker doesn't continually vacuum up valuable time, many project proposers avoid The Checker for other reasons.

One reason is that some project proposers are afraid The Checker will actually find a major fault in the project. If this is your fear, then please find another line of work! If there is truly some major unknown fault in your proposed project, it's far better to have The Checker discover it first rather than BigShot. And it's far better for <u>someone</u> (anyone!) to find such a fault before your company wastes the shareholder's dollars on implementing a dud.

If there is a risk you/your team knows about but would rather not discuss, you're still better off discussing it with The Checker instead of merely hoping BigShot won't notice the risk. Be proactive on this, not reactive. Better to discuss ways to mitigate the risk than to ignore it altogether—you'll be seen as a more valuable team player.

The second reason I believe some project proposers try to avoid The Checker is because they incorrectly believe The Checker will try to steal the thunder of the proposal. This is not likely. Why? Because most Checkers are risk-adverse.

They will not willingly put themselves directly in your shoes and take the risk of presenting a proposal that could be shot down by BigShot. They'd really rather just keep on collecting data, data, and more data!

My Recommendation

So, you have two choices when Encountering The Checker: One choice is to ignore/avoid The Checker. I don't recommend this. It sends up a red flag in The

Checker's mind that there must be a major fault(s) in the project that you don't want The Checker to find. The Checker will therefore do everything in his/her power to prevent you from reaching BigShot.

Even if you get time on Mr./Ms. BigShot's calendar, you'll likely find during your presentation that The Checker has proceeded you, and informally warned BigShot against your proposal. Now you'll be paddling upstream!

The other choice is to find a balanced approach in working with The Checker. This is my recommendation. Realize that Checkers do have a job to perform, get them the relevant data they need, but do take a subtle control of the process so that you don't forever spin your wheels simply supplying data, data, and more data.

You will need to help The Checker complete the project puzzle by eventually pointing them (repeatedly) to the benefits of the project, once their need for feature and function data has been *mostly* fulfilled. (I'm convinced that Checkers never actually reach their Nirvana—data overload!)

Then, let it be known to The Checker that you appreciate all s/he has done for you/your project (okay, so sometimes it's a bit of a stretch), and that you intend to make him/her "A Hero" in Mr./Ms. BigShot's eyes during your proposal presentation. Tell The Checker that you plan to mention to BigShot how helpful and diligent The Checker has been in ensuring that the final project proposal is thorough and complete.

Done at the right time, The Checker should then finally stand aside. (Though perhaps somewhat reluctantly—after all, s/he believes there is still a need for a little more data!) Then, follow-through and do make him/her "A Hero" in BigShot's eyes in the manner you said you would. This will smooth the way for you down the road…both in project implementation and in your next proposal.

Oh, some of you don't think there will be a "next proposal"? I think you're wrong. Once it becomes known that you were able to present successfully to BigShot, you'll be asked to present yet another proposal…and then another…and then another…

The Best Proposal Trick I Know

Here is the most powerful proposal trick I know: Give Mr./Ms. BigShot multiple choices.

You see, most proposers simply give BigShot a "Yes/No" presentation on an idea. This can be dangerous if BigShot perceives (rightly or wrongly) that s/he is merely being asked to "rubber stamp" a decision someone else has already made.

Remember that Mr./Ms. BigShot believes s/he has a responsibility to the company's shareholders to personally investigate each idea or suggestion that may lead to Shareholder Value. S/he wants to feel the thrill of having led a decision-making process, not simply "rubber stamping" someone else's work.

Mr./Ms. BigShot's desire to personally add value reminds me of a story I heard in my college Home Ec class about the introduction of boxed cake mixes. (Hang in here with me on this.)

The Boxed Cake Mix Example

When boxed cake mixes were initially introduced to a test market, all the homemaker had to do was add water to the mix and then bake the cake. The taste test results were fine—the participants liked the taste results. But the homemakers complained that the process was actually too easy…they wanted to personally add a bit more value to baking a cake for their family or friends.

The box mix developers therefore decided to purposely complicate the process by altering the cake mix so it required the addition of an egg(s) and oil or margarine/butter by the homemaker.

The results were quite interesting. Most taste test participants couldn't taste any difference between the cake made with just the mix and water vs. the cake made with the mix and additional ingredients included by the homemaker. But the homemakers overwhelmingly preferred the *process* where they had to do a bit more work. To this day, we still add the extra ingredients to our boxed cake mixes, brownie mixes, etc.

I think this same philosophy holds with many Big Shots. They want to feel that they have had more of a personal part in the decision process instead of saying merely "Yes" or "No".

Multiple Courses of Action

Therefore, a much better approach than "yes/no" is to give Mr./Ms. BigShot a choice of at least three courses of action. Four or five choices is also fine, but any more than that is too complicated.

I once presented a slate of eight choices. Though the recommended project course of action was eventually selected, I'll never present that many choices again. Mr. BigShot spent so much time and effort trying to keep the choices straight in his mind that it distracted from the decision making process.

Anyhow, let's say we're going to present three choices to Mr./Ms. BigShot. The first choice is usually a "do nothing differently" choice. The second choice is a proposal for a new course of action (different widget, service, process). The third choice is a proposal for a slightly different course of action.

The third proposed choice could simply be a different timeframe of what is proposed in the second choice—implementing something faster or in a more drawn out timeframe. Or, it could be a similar proposal to the second choice, but utilizing a different vendor's product/service.

Remember the Proper Focus

Not only are the resulting financial differences important, but also any differing risks between the three choices. Remember to focus on Shareholder Value benefits. Back off on enumerating features and functions, unless asked to do so by BigShot.

Some people balk when I suggest a first alternative of "do nothing differently." And yet, in most cases, it is indeed a viable option. Even if it isn't viable (say, because of new legal regulations), it still provides a very good comparison base for the two other proposals. It starts everyone off on the "same page" and, assuming it's handled correctly, will easily build rapport between BigShot, others in the room, and you as the presenter.

Present Neutrally

Here is the key tactical strategy to using this multiple choice approach. You will need to present all three alternatives in a neutral manner. By this, I mean present each as a truly viable option. Don't repeatedly press your particular choice. Let BigShot reach his/her own conclusion. Of course, if you are asked for your recommendation, feel free to politely give it— but don't push.

Big Shots love to convince themselves that they have made the decision on their own. And, that it is the right decision given his/her "investigation" of the information. Take advantage of this desire by presenting choices as truly viable alternatives. Ensure you have provided all the Shareholder Value pieces necessary for Mr./Ms. BigShot to complete the puzzle.

Perhaps a Surprise

There is a little surprise in pushing yourself to present three or more options. Sometimes—not very often, but sometimes—you will find a better course of action by forcing yourself to think of a third alternative. I know this, because it happened to me.

I once asked the project's engineer to help me come up with a third alternative for a large project requiring a three year nationwide implementation. The engineer suggested we propose rolling-out the project in two years instead of three. We both figured that the accelerated option would result in lower financial benefit because of all the overtime pay that would be required for the engineers and installers to do three years of work in just two years.

But a funny thing happened. When I put the accelerated timeframe into the complex financial model, the overall financial result was better, not worse. How could that be? There was all that extra overtime involved.

However, the model pointed out that all the front-line labor saving benefits from implementing the project one year earlier more than compensated for the overtime pay needed for a few engineers and installers.

By pushing ourselves to come up with a third alternative, we saved the company several million dollars. No kiddin'! The project was approved with our newly recommended advanced timing option. The financial gains were indeed realized as predicted. Advanced service was brought to the customers one year earlier. And, as you can imagine, the engineer and I were both on Cloud 9 for quite some time!

Chapter 9

Presenting a Polished Image

This will be a frustrating section for a few people. I hope you're not one of them. But if you are, then you and I will simply have to professionally agree to disagree. I feel very strongly about this section.

Research has shown <u>repeatedly</u> that dress and grooming matter—big time—in all but a very few high-tech companies. It matters more than it should, perhaps, but that's life. I suggest you learn to deal with it, as I had to, if you haven't done so already.

It has been shown that most people in the business world dress for failure. Even when they are trying to look their best, most men and women miss the mark. Why? Because they haven't learned what impresses Big Shots as a polished, professional image.

Though many men could benefit greatly by following the results of research conducted repeatedly over the past 30 years, it is actually women who have the most to gain. This isn't just Kathy O'Neal saying this from her experience. This is backed by years of research, and the confirmed options of thousands of executives…including the Big Shots!

Research shows that when a woman dresses appropriately for success, it does not guarantee success—but if she dresses inappropriately, it almost ensures failure. Let me repeat: When a woman dresses inappropriately, it almost ensures failure.

A Double Standard

Dressing inappropriately does not destroy a man's career to the same degree it does a woman's IF he is really good at what he does. Some men can move up in spite of a poor image. However, if a woman dresses inappropriately, she will be eliminated from promotional consideration by most male and female managers.

Research has shown a clear double standard. It certainly isn't fair, but it is reality. Women, I recommend that you not only learn to deal with it, but actually prosper by it.

Regardless of which gender you are, get the edge by learning the secrets to truly dressing for success…not only for your proposal presentation, but for you everyday office environment as well. And, that includes Casual Fridays, if your company has them.

Dress for Success Books

I highly recommend that you obtain the latest primer on dressing for your gender by John T. Molloy. For men, an updated version of the infamous 1975 Dress for Success came out in 1988, and is called New Dress for Success.

For women, John T. Malloy's mid-1970's research has been updated by the New Women's Dress for Success book, published in 1996. I've read both woman's books cover to cover. The research results are quite consistent, despite the 20 year time span. The right woman's business suit still wins hands down, despite the brief popularity of business dresses in the early 1990's. This doesn't really surprise me, though. My own experience has taught me much the same thing.

My Experience

It was 1981 when I remarked to a male colleague that I was frustrated by the lack of progress (promotions) in my management career. He suggested I try dressing differently. This was an interesting suggestion coming from him, since he was a somewhat casual dresser himself. I was a supervisor in a factory at the time, and one of the few female supervisors actually on the shop floor. I most often wore a clean, pressed blouse and skirt in bright colors.

My colleague mentioned that a researcher famous for a man's dress for success book had recently come out with a similar book for women. My friend didn't know what was recommended for women, but thought I should check it out.

I did check it out. Implementing the recommendations from that book ignited <u>my</u> revolution of <u>my</u> career. I took charge, and I soon prospered.

Why Most Women Fail

I was very fortunate to have a male colleague who took the risk to suggest to me that I should consider changing the way I dressed. The main reason that most women "dress for failure" is that none of their superiors tell them when they are dressed inappropriately.

Most male managers are afraid to tell a woman she is wearing something inappropriate, especially in our current politically correct age. Most women in management do not think it is their job to tell another female how to dress.

As a result, many women make the same mistakes over and over when dressing for work. There is no "old girl's club" in which senior women go out of their way to help their younger sisters.

When young men are not dressing appropriately, they are often told so by a male colleague. The wall of silence for females puts women at a tremendous disadvantage.

Why Most Men Fail

Dressing appropriately is also tricky for men. Most men also dress for failure. And not just those in ill-fitting polyester suits or garish ties. Most conservatively dressed men also dress in ways that severely hurt their careers.

How? John T. Molloy's research is overwhelming. The chief reasons most businessmen dress for failure is:

- They let their wives or girlfriends choose their clothing. (Hey, given most women dress for failure, this failure shouldn't be a surprise.)

- They let their favorite sales clerk or image consultant choose their clothing.

- They allow their background to dictate their clothing choices.

How to Dress for Success with Big Shots

There is a way for both men and women to choose to dress for success with Big Shots. Let time-tested research choose your clothing. Not Kathy O'Neal nor John T. Molloy's *personal* opinions of what looks good…but rather, what John T. Molloy's research shows. And, what Kathy O'Neal's experience (and the experience of many other successful professionals) has confirmed.

Hey, I personally happen to prefer business dresses with matching jackets for women. I find them very practical and I think they look very business-like. But guess what…most Big Shots don't agree with me. So you can rest assured that when it really counted— like my boss coming to town, or when I had to go to Headquarters to present a proposal—Kathy O'Neal brought out the appropriate business suit.

You know, whenever I mention John T. Molloy, there is usually one in every group who snickers and

<u>says</u> s/he has read his book, but insists s/he isn't going to follow one man's personal opinion. At that point, I just grin and say, "You obviously didn't read the first part of the book. The research results aren't Molloy's personal opinions. They are the opinions of the executives—including those Big Shots with the power to decide whether your proposal will get funded or not."

If you skipped over the introductory/research method sections of Molloy's book(s), you missed the main thrust. I strongly suggest you go back and correct your oversight…try implementing what the research clearly shows…or perhaps be forever doomed to wallow in frustration as to why the Big Shots aren't taking you seriously.

For Casual Work Environments

The finding that surprised Molloy's most recent researchers was that dress counted most for those who work in casual environments. (Remember my experience in the factory environment? It doesn't get much more casual than that!)

The impact of the wrong dress for "Casual Fridays", especially for women, calls for a heightened awareness in choosing your outfits especially on those days.

Good News

The good news is that anyone who starts to dress for success has an immediate measurable statistical advantage over his/her peers with respect to promotion (just in case promotions are important to you)—in some cases doubling his/her chances.

A professional image really counts when you only have a few seconds to grab BigShot's attention, and make a good first impression. The key to being credible is not creating any visual surprises. You do not want to wear the latest fashion or a new look that no one has ever seen. Remember that Mr./Ms. BigShot needs to have confidence in you personally—and you don't want to cause any distraction by wearing a "failure" outfit. Walk in the door looking like the polished professional you are!

An Outfit Example for Men

Though I really want to give you an example of an appropriate male outfit for a presentation, I find that, alas, there is no one single outfit that will work with all men in all regions of the USA in all situations.

For example, let's take the solid dark gray wool suit. Here is what Molloy's research has shown (quoted from page 63 of his New Dress for Success):

> **"Solid Dark Gray**: this is a strong positive with the upper middle class, a negative with the lower middle class. It is excellent for large men and negative for small men. It is good for heavy men, neutral on thin men. Before the public it is excellent, as it is on television. If you are a weak authority figure, use it. If you are a strong authority figure, it is neutral. If you are going to be

dealing with high-powered executives that you have never met, and you have no idea of their backgrounds or style, it is your safest choice."

Okay, so you get the point…you really need to get the book, and select the recommendations that best fit your own situation. Just a quick summary on shirts: Safest to pick solid white—in either all cotton, or a cotton/polyester blend with at least 50% cotton.

No bow ties! Buy a good silk tie in the proper length for you. If you are wearing a solid dark gray suit and a white shirt, try either a solid maroon tie (all solids—suit, shirt, and tie—are quite acceptable in the right colors) or a maroon tie with small white dots or small traditional foulard. It's a safe bet.

Lots of other good looking combinations are possible, and many correct combinations are actually pictured in Molloy's book. I paid $13.99 (US) for the paperback version of the book in early 2002—what a bargain for you men!

An Outfit Example for Women

There is an additional trick for women dressing to present to Mr./Ms. BigShot. For women presenters, the gender of Mr./Ms. BigShot can make a difference.

If presenting to a female Big Shot, try a <u>collarless</u> (i.e. no lapels) version of a traditional wool suit in medium to dark blue, navy, or medium to dark gray, with a white businesslike blouse that is feminine but not frilly. Pair this with simple, elegant jewelry—a string of pearls and matching "button" pearl earrings is quite safe. Further accessorize with plain pumps, a subdued wristwatch, and a gold or silver pen. Your look will be rich, elegant, upper class, and confident.

If presenting to a male Big Shot, you want to look "feminine but formidable." Go with the collared (i.e. with lapels) traditional wool suit in dark blue, navy, or medium to dark gray. The skirt should fall just below the knee and the jacket should hang six to eight inches below the waist. (Don't go with a short jacket—it doesn't test well. Too bad, as I personally like the shorter jackets on women under 5'4" like me.) Stick with the same type of white blouse, jewelry, and accessories as noted above, and you should be just fine.

As with the men's ability to dress for success, there are lots of other fine combinations, depending upon your body size and the gender/level of the person you are presenting to. Please get Molloy's New Women's Dress for Success if you don't already have it. I paid $13.99 (US) for my paperback copy in mid-2001, and consider it worth its weight in gold.

Chapter 10

Be Prepared! You May Need This Skill Set

Presenting a large, complex proposal may entail a skill set not often considered…table manners. No kiddin'. Sometimes you'll find yourself having a meal with Mr./Ms. BigShot either before or after your presentation. It hasn't happened very often to me, but it is best to "Be Prepared" by having polished dining skills.

My Mama

I was fortunate to have a mama who insisted her family use formal table manners on occasion. You see, when my sister and I were growing up, our father often worked late into the evening. So, it would usually be just my mama, sister and I for dinner.

This was in the early 1960's in "suburbia", and life in the USA was quickly becoming a lot less formal. We often ate dinner casually off TV trays in the living room while watching the Ed Sullivan Show.

The Beatles wanted to "Hold Your Hand" back then, Leslie Gore had a party where she would "Cry If I Want To", and there was a ventriloquist whose dummy in a box would always answer, "S'right!" (Ahhh, the good ol' days…)

Anyhow, my mama eventually became concerned about her daughters table manners…or lack thereof. So, she invented a game called "Your Queen's Manners". Once a month on our manners "game day," usually a Sunday, Mom would set a formal table in the dining room—no TV allowed! We would pretend that the Queen of England was coming to dine, and we wanted to make a good impression, of course!

Our mama would teach us how to use "Your Queen's Manners," such as breaking a dinner roll into four pieces, and buttering and eating each fourth separately…always placing the butter knife back down in the correct place. At first, it was fun.

But as we got older, Mom started adding complexity to the place settings…a funny looking fork, a wide soup spoon, another glass. When my sister and I got frustrated by all the new rules, our mama would simply smile and say, "But you never know when you'll be dining with the Queen—you must be prepared!"

By the time 1970 rolled around, I, as a "worldly 17-year old" had had it with "Your Queen's Manners," even though it still occurred only once a month. By that time, Mom had us using three different forks, three different knives, three different spoons, and a variety of goblets, glasses, plates and bowls.

I remember saying to my mama in total exasperation, "Mom, no one eats like this anymore. Even in a nice restaurant, there's no more complexity than two forks."

Mom just smiled and said, "But Kathy, you never know when you'll be dining with the Queen of England. You must be prepared!"

Fast Forward to the 1990's

Now let's fast forward to the 1990's. I, along with two Florida colleagues, have recently been promoted to Director level in our Fortune 100 company. We are so excited to be invited to our first fabled Financial Leadership Retreat. That's where the top financial folks from all around the country are brought together for two days in a wonderful lodge in a forest in Pennsylvania.

Before the more serious business of the second day, specialists are brought in the first day to provide us with "*advanced* teamwork skills" by having us play various games on the grounds of the lodge. It's all very casual, and actually a lot of fun getting to know others in a nice, relaxed atmosphere. We're all wearing our color coordinated team sweatshirts provided by the "*advanced* teamwork skills" specialists.

Imagine our surprise, therefore, when we're led into a beautiful formal dining room that evening for dinner. It is the most gorgeous dining room I have ever seen.

First Class Dining

There is a heavy chandelier suspended over each large, round table set for eight. Each table is softly draped with a white cloth, covered with a creamy lace overlay. Each large centerpiece consists of freshly cut flowers and three lit candles, which cause a rosy twinkling from the chandeliers above. We silently tread across the thickly padded, dense hunters' green carpet.

Being the "new kids" in the financial executive ranks, we three from Florida learn that we are going to be seated with Mr. BigShot—our Executive Vice President and Controller of the entire company. Only one level separates our BigShot from the CEO, so our BigShot is indeed a high powered player.

This is his first exposure to the three of us. He will soon be coming to Florida to hear two of us pitch him a multi-million dollar proposal. We therefore find ourselves unexpectedly thrust into a high-risk "opportunity". As we take our seats across from Mr. BigShot, I can see the look of sheer terror on my colleagues faces after they glance down briefly at the table.

The place settings consist of—you guessed it—three different forks, three different knives, three different spoons, three crystal goblets in varying sizes, and a myriad of plates and bowls. I can feel the fear flowing from my colleagues on either side of me. Which utensil goes with which food dish?

I, on the other hand, as the waiter lays the linen napkin across my lap, simply smile and say silently to myself, "Thank-you, mama!"

For you see, you never know when you'll be dining with the Queen of England...or even with your own Mr./Ms. BigShot. So, you'd better be prepared!

If your table manners (or other business manners and/or international protocol) need a bit of polishing, I recommend a little book called <u>Business Etiquette Mastery</u> by Joli Andre. As of this writing, it is available at amazon.com and via Ms. Andre's website: <u>www.polishedprofessionals.com</u>.

You know, the older I get, the more I find that sometimes my mama was right!

Chapter 11

Effective Display Tools & Presentation Tips

There comes the time when you'll need to decide whether you want to use any audio-visual (AV) aids, and if so, do you want to go high-tech, low-tech, or no-tech.

Some Big Shots have a definite feeling against certain AV aids. Some dislike overheads or slides...some are aggravated by the whir of the machinery if it is close by. Others are just tired of presentations which feature a huge stack of overheads and little else.

Don't use flip charts unless you write/spell well quickly while under pressure. Be careful about handouts becoming a distraction away from your proposal.

So what's a presenter to do?!?

Your BigShot's AV Likes/Dislikes

If possible, learn the likes/dislikes of your particular BigShot. For example, if Mr./Ms. BigShot is in a high-tech, cutting edge electronics display company, showing up with just handouts in a three ring binder likely won't cut it. A multi-media presentation on a lap-top projector might be what is expected.

On the other hand, I've heard some BigShots complain that if they see one more Power Point presentation, they'll scream. They just want a proposer to focus on a verbal discussion with them, with a couple of simple handouts.

If it's not possible for you to learn Mr./Ms. BigShot's AV likes/dislikes, then here are some general guidelines.

Visual Basics

Remember that Big Shots have an accelerated timeframe. They fear you are going to waste their time and/or are going to confuse them with technical jargon.

Big Shots want to be in control. (Hey, they are merely putting up with giving <u>you</u> the floor on the chance you might have a way to increase Shareholder Value!) Also remember that Mr./Ms. BigShot wants to participate in the decision-making process.

Therefore, keep any visuals very brief and to the point. Some people say 8 – 10 words per page. I say you can push it to a max of 5 lines per page, with no more than 5 words per line. But that's it.

Remember to focus on Benefits, and back off giving Features info unless asked for it.

If you are using a screen visual (overhead machine, slide projector), be sure that any relevant handouts are identical to what is on the screen.

Leave lots of white space on the handout for Mr./Ms. BigShot to take notes. If you are handing out more than four or five pages, consider providing a binder of some sort for easy storage.

Color has been proven to increase retention by more than 250%. Also, you may want to consider the use of two different types of visual media if your proposal is longer than 30 minutes.

Choose Your Tool(s)

Here are some pros and cons of the various tools available.

1. <u>Simple binder of handouts</u>. Very portable and no electricity required. No need to dim the lights and risk Mr./Ms. BigShot taking a nap. Great of you have highly developed verbal presentation skills. However, this method can give a low tech feel, which may/may not be an advantage. Also, this technique is best used with six or fewer total participants.

2. <u>Flip charts</u>. No electricity required and no need to dim the lights. Versatile. But, you must possess good and quick hand printing skills under pressure, and the ability to spell. Make sure when you talk, you are facing Mr./Ms. BigShot, not the flip chart. Have extra markers handy, and beware of bleed-through on thin paper. (You might want to bind double pages together ahead of time.)

3. <u>Overhead projector</u>. Good for an audience of over six participants. I like to add a word or two to the

transparency as I talk for an interactive feel. Easy for others to follow. Good for jumping forward or backward to answer questions. However, a screen is required, and the tool is electrical, which means it will hum and/or breakdown at the most inopportune times. The lights must usually be dimmed, so you therefore risk losing eye contact with Mr./Ms. BigShot. Overhead projectors sometimes have a dated "low tech" appearance if BigShot is used to seeing animated presentations.

4. <u>Laptop, computer-controlled presentations</u>. Great for high-tech, animated presentations. These can grab BigShot's attention if the visuals are properly constructed and paced. However, the learning and developing curves to produce the proposal this way may be lengthy. The computer can and will breakdown. It requires cables and connectors which disappear minutes before your presentation (so bring extras). If you are going to use this tool, I'd suggest having a back-up method such as an overhead machine with prepared transparencies... just in case Murphy's Law is encountered.

5. <u>Video-teleconferencing</u>. Very up-to-date, and has a much better image quality now than in the past decade. Given the terrorist attacks in the USA on 9/11/01, we're now being told that this is the wave of the future. I'm not so sure. These gizmos take a high investment and plenty of technical know-how. Unless you're in a company that supplies these devices/services, my guess is that Mr./Ms. BigShot

will still prefer a face-to-face proposal. What do you think?

Presentation Tips

Here are a few tips to help your proposal go smoothly.

<u>Do:</u>

- Watch the time discreetly, and keep things moving

- It's OK to use unobtrusive notes/index cards to keep you on track

- Gain/maintain eye contact with all participants

- Drink only water before/while presenting. Sodas have a tendency to close your throat, and juices may upset an already jittery stomach. I won't even comment about alcohol!

- Keep pen/paper handy to jot down follow-up needs

- Remember that occasional pauses can be effective.

- Restate a lengthy or complex question in your own terms. That will ensure you truly understand what is being asked, and will clarify the question in the minds of all participants.

Don't:

- Read verbatim from lengthy text on paper.

- Talk to the screen, chart, wall, projector, your shoes. Point/mark, turn to face BigShot, then speak.

- Interrupt a participant

- Use a laser pointer—it's irritating to many and considered unsafe if used incorrectly

- Hold a pointer after you've finished using it. (Many find any type of physical pointer irritating—you might instead just gesture briefly with your open hand.)

- Fiddle with your watch, bracelet, ring, hair, change in your pocket

- Exceed 90 minutes without a break

- Let The Checker, if present, divert the presentation with too many questions. Tell him/her you'll be glad to provide other information after the presentation to address his/her additional "interest". (If possible, don't use/repeat words like "concern" or "problem".)

Calming the Jitters

A little nervous? Good. A few nerves actually helps most presenters (including me) by giving them additional energy, which enlivens the presentation.

More than a few nerves? Okay, try some of these tactics:

- Get a full night's sleep the night before.

- Make sure you are thoroughly prepared and rehearsed.

- Check AV aids yet again.

- Take a deep breath and exhale slowly. Repeat several times.

- Stretch yourself up as though you were being pulled by a string attached to the top of your head. Imagine that you are taller than you actually are.

- I like to see the room where I'll be presenting well in advance—at a time when I can walk around it by myself, and get used to where I'll be standing for the presentation.

- Remember that the participants, especially Mr./Ms. BigShot, are usually your allies. They want you to succeed, and they honestly hope you have a wonderful proposal to share with them. So, think positively!

A Special Situation Calls for Creativity

I'm going to share with you another true story. I'm not recommending this method unless you have solid verbal skill sets and you find yourself in circumstances similar to these.

The proposal was for a high dollar investment in software to increase the efficiency of existing machinery, and the effectiveness of front-line people who used the machinery. This was in a customer service area with flat Revenue projections for the foreseeable future. That wasn't going to change.

The engineer and I had to present to the new BigShot. Mr. New BigShot had just come to the organization a few days earlier. He was spending his first four days on the job listening to his <u>eight</u> Vice Presidents go over their current and proposed engineering projects. Each Vice President got only a half-day to say what s/he wanted to say.

The engineer and I were scheduled for a meeting separately from our VP's because our project was so large and complex. We were given the last time slot of 45 minutes at the tail-end of the four days. The engineer figured we had been negatively placed there because some of the executives were confused as to why the company should even consider making a high-dollar investment in a service area with flat Revenue projections. Anyhow, all the VPs wanted to get their pitches in before ours.

My Challenge

The engineer gave me a challenge. Because we knew that Mr. New BigShot was to have four full days of nothing but slides, charts, and handouts, I was challenged by the engineer to come up with a financial presentation that didn't use anything like that.

"What, are you nuts?" I said. "How am I to do a financial presentation for this project proposal without slides, charts, or handouts?"

"I don't know," was the engineer's reply, "but I really think we'll do better if we just walk into this new guy's office and focus on using strong verbal skill sets."

Well, I couldn't argue with that logic. A verbal focus was likely best, given the circumstances. But what could I do to grab BigShot's attention, and convince him of the merit of the investment? It was already Tuesday afternoon, and we were scheduled to present that Thursday at 5 pm.

The 59¢ Yellow File Folder

I thought and thought. I was at home on Wednesday evening when I spied a couple of yellow file folders I had recently bought for another use. They were nice and bright, and had only cost 59¢ each. My gentle teaching methods kicked in.

What if I cut strips from one of the file folders to represent the annual total Revenue streams, then tore away the various Expenses to leave the Profit? It would be a classic high-level case of the old, simplistic formula:

Profit = Revenue – Expense (You do remember this, yes?)

So, that's exactly what I did. We were presenting three different options, including the first one of "do nothing differently." The second one required the investment in the first two years, and the third option showed what would happened if the investment was made all in the first year.

Because we were dealing with software expense, the investment really wasn't that big compared to the efficiency gains (and hence expense reductions) of the total financials for the area.

We two walked into New BigShot's office right at 5 pm on Thursday. He looked tired. He was surprised we hadn't brought an overhead projector and screen with us. The engineer explained to Mr. New BigShot we just wanted to talk directly to him without any AV aids. Mr. New BigShot brightened up, and invited us

Kathy O'Neal

to sit around a small coffee table in comfortable chairs.

The engineer spoke first, and talked for 20 minutes. So well prepared, the engineer required nothing more than an occasional glance at a single sheet of handwritten notes. Then, it was my turn for the financials.

"You've probably heard," I began, "that this service area has flat Revenue for the foreseeable future." New BigShot nodded his head.

"And you're probably wondering why the company should invest millions of dollars in software development for an area with flat Revenue," I continued.

"Yes, I was indeed wondering about that," he answered. The engineer had been right—executives had been talking negatively to Mr. New BigShot about our proposal before we even got there!

"I'm going to show you why," I said confidently. With that, I placed a row of 10 identical strips, each cut from that 59¢ yellow file folder, directly in front of him on the coffee table. "This," I explained, "depicts the flat Revenue dollar level for each of the next 10 years."

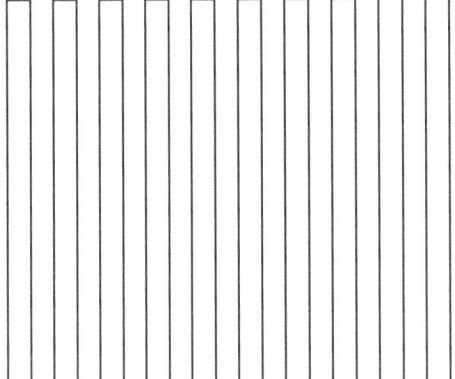

Shows the flat
Revenue dollars
projected for the next
10 years.

I remember that he had a dark wooden coffee table, and the bright yellow strips showed up really well. Do you think I grabbed his initial attention using this method to begin a financial presentation? You betcha!

The Beginning of "Do Nothing Differently"

Next, I picked up the first strip, and tore it precisely at a point I had marked in pencil on the back of the strip. "This top piece," I remarked, "is the amount of the Revenue dollars that currently has to be used to pay the Labor expense for this area." I placed both torn pieces back down where the whole strip used to be. The remaining nine strips were then torn in the same manner. The result looked like this:

Top section represents the amount of the total Revenue dollars used to pay for the Labor expense.

Next, I picked up the lower section of the first strip. Again, I tore it at a point I had marked on the back. Returning those pieces back down into place, the first year was now divided into three pieces. "This middle section," I said, "represents the amount of all the other Expense utilized in this operation." Tearing the other nine strips in a similar manner, I concluded, "You can see that there is a small amount of Profit left each year, after taking out all the Labor Expense and Other Expenses from the Revenue."

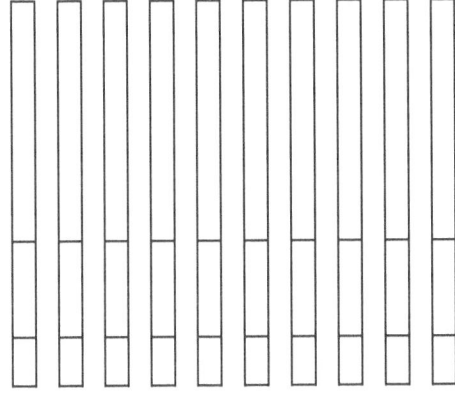

The top section shows the amount of Revenue dollars used to pay Labor expense.

The middle section shows the amount of Revenue dollars used to pay all Other expense.

The bottom section shows the remaining dollars of Profit.

Pointing to the bottom row of pieces, I said, "If we Do Nothing Differently, the amount of Profit we will have is shown by the bottom section. Not bad, but not stellar." Mr. New BigShot agreed.

The Development of a Second Course of Action

At this point, I laid out a fresh line of 10 full strips, again representing the flat Revenue dollars projected for the next 10 years. Picking up the first strip, I again tore off and referenced the amount of Revenue dollars that would have to be used to pay for the Labor expense. The bottom piece was again torn to show the amount of Revenue dollars used for all the usual Other expenses.

The remaining stub for Profit, however, was torn in half for that first year. Why? Because that was the amount of the usual Profit that could instead be put into developing software for a New Course of Action.

We called it a Second Course of Action Alternative to the first Do Nothing Differently.

The second year of Second Course of Action Alternative showed two interesting things. First, another investment amount, similar to the investment amount in the first year, would be needed to finish up the software development. Secondly, the software developed in the first year would start to have the desired impact of reducing the Labor expenses in the second year. After the software was fully developed at the end of the second year, the full desired impact of the Labor expense reduction would quickly become notable. As the need for Labor expense goes down, guess what happens to the Profit level?

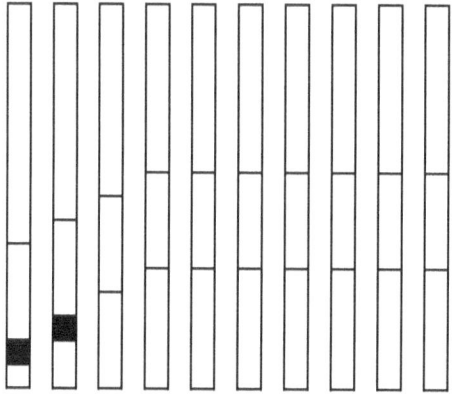

The top section shows the amount of Revenue dollars needed to pay Labor expense.

The middle section shows the amount of Revenue dollars used to pay all Other expense, except for the new Software expense, shown in black in Yrs. 1 and 2.

The bottom section shows the remaining dollars of Profit.

Hey, not a bad increase in Profit … even for an area with flat Revenue!

The Development of a Third Course of Action

For the Third Course of Action Alternative, we showed what would happen if the company was willing to take all the Profit in Year 1, and put it towards the software development in that timeframe. That meant that the reduction in Labor expense would be realized even sooner. What do you suppose that would do to the overall amount of Profit?

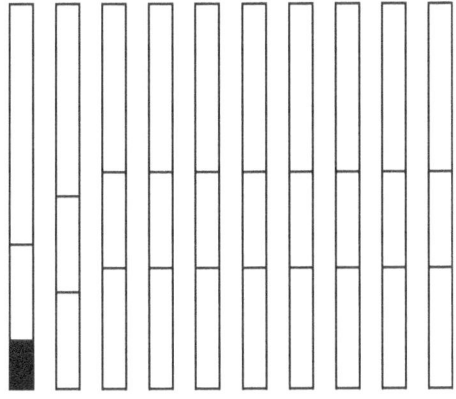

The top section shows the amount of Revenue dollars needed to pay Labor expense.

The middle section shows the amount of Revenue dollars used to pay all Other expense, except for the new Software expense, shown in black in Yr. 1.

The bottom section shows the remaining dollars of Profit.

Though a bit hard to see here, the total Profit from the Third Course of Action Alternative is the highest— about 5% higher than the Second Alternative.

Either new course of action would result in more than doubling the amount of Profit in that area. Do you think New BigShot was interested?

Do you think New BigShot now gave a flip about whether the Revenues were flat? Heck, no! Do you think New BigShot cared why the software would cost so much to develop? Nope.

Mr. New BigShot was a smart man—he knew the real name of the game is Profit. He was easily able to complete the puzzle—just like you did, didn't you?

Which of the three courses of action do you think Mr. New BigShot picked? I'll never forget it. He simply pointed to the bottom section of the Third Course of Action Alternative, and said, "I want that!"

The engineer and I nonchalantly responded, "Okay, we'll get started on that Third Course of Action." We left his office <u>elated</u> and walked back to our respective desks. The entire presentation for this multi-million dollar proposal had taken just 40 minutes.

My Boss' Reaction

By the time I got back to my desk, it was 5:45 pm. I started packing up my things to go home. Then, I got a call from my boss, Phil.

"What exactly did you do in the proposal presentation to Mr. New BigShot?" he asked. Phil had already seen my presentation before with the charts & graphs, and had naturally assumed I would use those same tools. I hadn't wanted to scare Phil with the engineer's off-the-wall plan for no AV aids...Phil could get a little too uptight at times, even though he was overall a pretty good boss.

Hmmm, Phil sounded a little tense. Gee, I thought the presentation had gone pretty well. "Why do you ask?" I queried.

My boss explained, "Because Mr. New BigShot just called up here and said he learned more from you and the engineer in 40 minutes than he'd learned in the past four days from all of his eight VPs combined. So I'm begging you to tell me…just what exactly did you do?"

"Well, Phil," I said, "it all started with a 59¢ yellow file folder…"

Chapter 12

Success! Now What?

Congratulations! You've made it through your presentation, or through this booklet, or both. Now what?

First of all, if Mr./Ms. BigShot didn't select the project alternative you thought was best, don't take it personally. S/he may have additional information you aren't aware of. Or, s/he could have flat out made a wrong decision. Big Shots are human, too, and wrong decisions are made. (Remember the Alto!)

Second of all, you must personally ensure that any follow-up requests are promptly handled—including those from The Checker. Do what you promised, and keep in contact if the project did get funded. If possible, maintain contact with Mr./Ms. BigShot as the project progresses—very brief progress reports (no more than one page) on occasion would likely be appreciated.

Think in terms of partnerships—with The Checkers and the Big Shots, and any other participants of your business world.

Get ready emotionally for yet another presentation in the future. Once the word gets around that you were successful in presenting to Mr./Ms. BigShot (whether s/he selected your recommended course of action or not), you'll soon find yourself being asked to represent other people or groups who have proposals to offer. What a nice compliment!

Get ready emotionally for perhaps new leadership opportunities. Now that you've been in a highly visible position, your name just may be on the lips of the executives. If a new leadership position comes your way, fantastic! Don't get scared. Fear not! Accelerated help is on the way—just check out our website and <u>free</u> newsletters for ongoing information on Leadership, Productivity, and Presentations. Full contact information is given at the end of this book.

Please consider sharing your own presentation tips, tricks, tactics and techniques. Let me know what worked and what didn't work for you by dropping me an e-mail at: <u>kathy@accelerated-manager.com</u>

I'll regularly send out tidbits in the newsletters on what has been helpful in accelerating people's careers. Perhaps you'd like to have your success story considered for inclusion?

If you've found the information in this booklet helpful, and know of a group or organization that would benefit from a presentation of this material, please be aware that in addition to being an author, I am also a professional speaker. Having presented to companies and groups of all sizes, I also have international experience as well. For more information, just call me at 321-939-0982 from 10 am – 5:30 pm EST, Monday – Friday.

Though it may be hard in today's pressure-filled business world, remember to always tell the truth. Honesty and integrity really do have the upper hand over the long haul. Manage for the common good—

the company, its customers, employees, and shareholders.

And remember the Alto…

§

"None of us can claim perfection and few can wear the mantle of hero or heroine, but each of us has the option of choosing a life of decency and self-discipline, self-reliance and diligence. From time to time, we fail our own standards, but our standards will never fail us."

—Elizabeth Dole

Crossword Puzzle

Across

2 Focus on (<u>10 across</u>), not (<u>2 across</u>).
4 Some say _____-teleconferencing is the wave of the future.
5 Present multiple choices or _____ of action.
7 _____ charts require good handwriting under stress.
9 A seldom used, but powerful tactic is gentle _____.
10 (See 2 across)
12 Maintain _____ contact with all participants.
15 Big Shots focus on _____ Value.
16 Don't set false _____.
17 Kathy O'Neal is an author and professional _____.
18 Remember the _____!
19 Do choose an _____ attitude.
21 Many Big Shots are not that good with detailed _____.
22 In a Hewlett Packard division, (<u>22 across</u>)/(<u>2 down</u>) faces were sometimes used in financial presentations.
24 Profit = Revenue - _____
26 Big Shots seek people with (<u>34 across</u>) and (<u>26 across</u>).
27 Participants, especially Mr./Ms. BigShot, are usually your _____.

28 _____'s Law is often encountered with laptop, computer-controlled presentations.

29 The first of multiple choices presented is often "Do Nothing _____."

31 Manage for the _____ good.

33 Tell The Checker you'll be glad to provide other information after the presentation to address his/her additional _____.

34 (See 26 across)

Down

1 Don't exceed 90 _____ without a break.

2 (See 22 across)

3 Do make noticeable ___ improvements.

6 Big Shots' Fear #1: You are going to _____ his/her time.

8 Your job is to _____ all the pieces necessary for BigShot to complete the puzzle.

11 Do make a great first _____.

13 The _____ loves data, data, and more data.

14 Fear not! _____ help is on the way.

20 Be prepared! You may need polished _____ skills.

23 Drink only _____ before/during a presentation.

25 Speak, write and _____ well.

30 Even when they are trying to look their best, most people in the business world dress for _____.

32 The older I get, the more I find that sometimes my _____ was right.

Kathy O'Neal

About the Author/Contact Us

Kathy O'Neal is a seasoned Fortune 100 Director, expert business woman, and experienced international speaker and author. She is a corporate veteran with over 20 years experience at AT&T, managing groups as large as 185 people.

In addition, Kathy has received much acclaim for her ability to "pitch" high-dollar project proposals to top decision makers. Over $1.1 Billion to date has been granted to project proposals presented by Kathy.

Representing AT&T regarding its win of the prestigious Malcolm Baldrige national quality award, Kathy has presented to Fortune 1000 companies such as Bristol-Myers Squibb, Travelers Insurance, American Century, and Whirlpool Financial:

> *"Again, my special thanks to you for taking time from your busy schedule to speak to our Leadership Conference. Your presentation was enlightening, your delivery was sparkling, and your message had a positive impact on our conference."*

> *James E. LeBlanc*
> *Chairman and CEO*
> *Whirlpool Financial Corp.*

Kathy is the founder of both the Accelerated Career Research & Development Group and the Accelerated Manager Development Group. Accelerated Career R&D Group focuses on individual self-development, while the Accelerated Manager Development Group focuses on developing groups of managers and other professionals within corporations.

Graduating with straight A's, Kathy was awarded a Masters of Business Administration (MBA) in 1991, with a major in Organizational Behavior/ Human Relations. She also holds a Bachelor of Science Degree in Mathematics, graduating on the Dean's Honor List. Kathy started her professional life as a high school mathematics instructor, switching to the business world after three years.

Email: kathy@accelerated-manager.com

Website: www.accelerated-manager.com

Phone: 321-939-0982 (Int'l dialing: 011-01)
Monday – Friday, 10 am – 5:30 pm, EST.

Fax: 888-628-9741

Address: PO Box 770655, Orlando, FL 32877-0655 (USA)

www.ingramcontent.com/pod-product-compliance
Lightning Source LLC
Chambersburg PA
CBHW030357290526
45785CB00004B/1795